THE
• Amazing Facts Book •
OF BIBLE PROMISES

FOREWORD BY
DOUG BATCHELOR

AMAZING FACTS

The Amazing Facts Book of Bible Promises
© Copyright 2016 by Amazing Facts
P.O. Box 1058
Roseville, CA 95490

Unless otherwise noted, Scripture taken from the New King James Version®. Copyright © 1982 by Thomas Nelson. Used by permission. All rights reserved.

Discover Amazing Facts at www.amazingfacts.org. Find more informative, life-changing Christian books, magazines, DVDs, and more at afbookstore.com.

Compiled and written by Laurie Lyon
Edited by Steven Winn
Cover by Haley Trimmer
Layout by Greg Solie • AltaGraph

ISBN: 978-1-58019-647-5

Foreword

In 2013, a Northern California husband and wife were out for a leisurely stroll with their dog when they spotted the end of a rusted can sticking out of the dirt on their property. Stopping to investigate, they found, to their astonishment, that the can contained dozens of solid gold coins from the 1800s. Searching further, they found more rusty cans filled with gold coins, all in nearly mint condition.

Known as the Saddle Ridge Hoard, it was valued at over $10 million and is one of the greatest treasure troves ever discovered in the United States. Amazingly, the treasure had sat there for years, undiscovered, right in their own backyard!

It makes you wonder how many of us today are overlooking the much greater treasure trove of genuine happiness, joy, and peace that can be found only through the Word of God and a trusting relationship with our Creator.

God yearns to guide and comfort you today, and this book is designed to

~ BOOK OF BIBLE PROMISES ~

help you quickly find His encouragement regarding your particular situations.

I pray that you will be blessed as you come to trust in the One who freely offers you His wisdom and His "exceedingly great and precious promises" (2 Peter 1:4) and who wants to enter into a saving relationship with you today. You can count on Him to provide all the encouragement, strength, and hope you need for all of life's journey.

The many ministries of Amazing Facts focus on turning people's attention to God's Word. If you enjoy this little promise book, you'll certainly appreciate the epic treasures of truth you can discover at our many Bible websites — see page 138 for a list. These websites offer hundreds of free online resources, including fascinating Bible studies, books, and videos. Additionally, most of our websites even allow you to respond with Bible questions and prayer requests.

We hope to see you there!

Pastor Doug Batchelor
President, Amazing Facts

~ Table of Contents ~

Peace 7
Encouragement 13
Grace 19
Self-worth 27
Strength 35
Wisdom 41
Anger 47
Anxiety 55
Distant 61
Scared 69
Worry About the Future 75
Grief 83
Guilt 89
The Weight of the World 95
Loneliness 103
Hitting Rock Bottom 109
Stress 117
Temptation 125
When No One Cares 131

Websites of Bible Truth 138
More Resources 140

Bible Promises for When You Need
Peace

So many circumstances in our world—even day-to-day events—can leave you feeling distressed and frazzled. Peace is one of the gifts of the Spirit of God, and sometimes it may seem to be one of the most elusive. But God wants to change that. He desires to enter your heart and mind and bring you lasting peace! Read and savor His promises to you ...

When You Need Peace

"You will keep him in perfect peace, whose mind is stayed on You, because he trusts in You."

~ Isaiah 26:3 ~

Focusing daily on the Lord and trusting Him to direct your life will allow Him to create His peace in you.

"Oh, that you had heeded My commandments! Then your peace would have been like a river."

~ Isaiah 48:18 ~

Peace comes as a natural result of obedience to the law of God.

When You Need Peace

"And His name will be called Wonderful, Counselor, Mighty God, Everlasting Father, Prince of Peace."

~ Isaiah 9:6 ~

Always remember that Jesus is your Source of genuine peace!

"Then He arose and rebuked the wind, and said to the sea, 'Peace, be still!'"

~ Mark 4:39 ~

The same Lord who calmed the savage storm longs to do the same in your life.

WHEN YOU NEED PEACE

"For He Himself is our peace, who has made both one, and has broken down the middle wall of separation."

~ Ephesians 2:14 ~

God, the ultimate peacemaker, can reconcile even those with "impossible" differences.

"Peace I leave with you, My peace I give to you; not as the world gives do I give to you."

~ John 14:27 ~

The superficial, short-lived "peace" of this world comes when everything seems to go your way, but it can't hold a candle to the all-encompassing peace of Christ that lasts for eternity!

WHEN YOU NEED PEACE

"These things I have spoken to you,
that in Me you may have peace.
In the world you will have
tribulation; but be of good cheer,
I have overcome the world."

~ John 16:33 ~

*By remaining in Jesus Christ, you can find
the peace that transcends any troubles
you may experience in this world.*

"Therefore, having been justified
by faith, we have peace with God
through our Lord Jesus Christ."

~ Romans 5:1 ~

*Through His sacrifice, Jesus has made it
possible for us to be reconciled to God,
to be at peace with Him, and that is the
most vital and lasting peace we can have.*

When You Need Peace

"In everything by prayer and supplication, with thanksgiving, let your requests be made known to God; and the peace of God, which surpasses all understanding, will guard your hearts and minds through Christ Jesus."

~ Philippians 4:6, 7 ~

Go to God with all your needs and He will provide you with a peace that is even beyond comprehension!

. . . .

The Lord of peace invites you to lay your burdens at His feet. Give Him your frantic schedule, family disputes, financial troubles, and anything else that disquiets your soul. Trust in the ultimate Peacemaker and allow Him to rule in your life today!

BIBLE PROMISES FOR WHEN YOU NEED
Encouragement

It happens to us all at one time or another. Life comes crashing in, weighing us down with burdens and cares of all kinds. It's easy to give in to our emotions, but it isn't the healthiest response—or the most helpful. If you're feeling overwhelmed by life, read and absorb these promises from your heavenly Father, precious reminders of His deep, never-ending love and concern for you!

WHEN YOU NEED ENCOURAGEMENT

"Though I walk in the midst of trouble, You will revive me; You will stretch out Your hand against the wrath of my enemies, and Your right hand will save me."

~ Psalm 138:7 ~

Whatever troubles perplex you in this life, God is always close at hand, reaching out to deliver you.

"Be of good courage, and He shall strengthen your heart, all you who hope in the LORD."

~ Psalm 31:24 ~

In any situation, God will give you courage from above if you put your trust in Him.

WHEN YOU NEED ENCOURAGEMENT

"The eternal God is your refuge, and underneath are the everlasting arms; He will thrust out the enemy from before you, and will say, 'Destroy!'"

~ Deuteronomy 33:27 ~

There could be no better refuge than the all-powerful God of the universe whose strong but gentle arms will always support and defend you without fail!

"He gives power to the weak, and to those who have no might He increases strength"

~ Isaiah 40:29 ~

Though this world often saps your strength, God is an unwavering source of power.

WHEN YOU NEED ENCOURAGEMENT

"Peace I leave with you, My peace I give to you; not as the world gives do I give to you. Let not your heart be troubled, neither let it be afraid."

~ John 14:27 ~

Jesus will provide His peace to enable you to rise above any challenge.

"Being confident of this very thing, that He who has begun a good work in you will complete it until the day of Jesus Christ."

~ Philippians 1:6 ~

It is God's intention to save you for eternity; He won't give up on you!

WHEN YOU NEED ENCOURAGEMENT

"Therefore humble yourselves under the mighty hand of God, that He may exalt you in due time, casting all your care upon Him, for He cares for you"

~ 1 Peter 5:6, 7 ~

Trust that God is guiding you and wants you to place all your worries into His capable hands.

"Let us run with endurance the race that is set before us, looking unto Jesus, the author and finisher of our faith"

~ Hebrews 12:1, 2 ~

Jesus, the Author of your faith, will give you all the stamina you need to carry you through.

WHEN YOU NEED ENCOURAGEMENT

"For I am persuaded that neither death nor life, nor angels nor principalities nor powers, nor things present nor things to come, nor height nor depth, nor any other created thing, shall be able to separate us from the love of God which is in Christ Jesus our Lord."

~ Romans 8:38, 39 ~

Nothing can separate you from His love—it's impossible!

. . . .

Be encouraged in the knowledge that God is with you always and His love for you is rock solid!

Bible Promises for When You Need
His Grace

Every one of us has broken God's law. Whether you've strayed unintentionally or with rebellion in your heart, there is a path to forgiveness and reconciliation with the Lord. Read these assurances from His Word ...

WHEN YOU NEED HIS GRACE

"Surely He scorns the scornful,
but gives grace to the humble."

~ Proverbs 3:34 ~

*It's a good starting point when
you recognize and admit that
you need God's help.*

"But God demonstrates His own love
toward us, in that while we were
still sinners, Christ died for us."

~ Romans 5:8 ~

*Even when you've turned away from
Him and gone your own way, Jesus has
immeasurable compassion toward you.*

WHEN YOU NEED HIS GRACE

"In Him we have redemption through His blood, the forgiveness of sins, according to the riches of His grace."

~ Ephesians 1:7 ~

It is only through Jesus that we can receive the grace of God.

"For all have sinned and fall short of the glory of God, being justified freely by His grace through the redemption that is in Christ Jesus, whom God set forth as a propitiation by His blood, through faith."

~ Romans 3:23–25 ~

Jesus paid the ultimate price so that, by trusting in Him, you can be made right with God.

When You Need His Grace

"If we confess our sins, He is faithful and just to forgive us our sins and to cleanse us from all unrighteousness."

~ 1 John 1:9 ~

If you admit your wrongdoing to God and turn away from it, He promises to wash it all away.

"Therefore, having been justified by faith, we have peace with God through our Lord Jesus Christ, through whom also we have access by faith into this grace in which we stand, and rejoice in hope of the glory of God."

~ Romans 5:1, 2 ~

Because of what Christ has done, you can have real hope for the future.

WHEN YOU NEED HIS GRACE

"May our Lord Jesus Christ Himself, and our God and Father, who has loved us and given us everlasting consolation and good hope by grace, comfort your hearts and establish you in every good word and work."

~ 2 Thessalonians 2:16, 17 ~

Receiving God's grace propels you into doing good works.

WHEN YOU NEED HIS GRACE

"But we believe that through the grace of the Lord Jesus Christ we shall be saved"

~ Acts 15:11 ~

When you receive His forgiveness you are also receiving the gift of eternal life.

"Now all things are of God, who has reconciled us to Himself through Jesus Christ, and has given us the ministry of reconciliation."

~ 2 Corinthians 5:18 ~

After forgiving you, God asks you to share the good news of His grace with others.

When You Need His Grace

> **"For sin shall not have dominion over you, for you are not under law but under grace."**
>
> ~ Romans 6:14 ~

When God forgives you, He also empowers you to begin living a victorious and obedient life for Him.

. . . .

Because Jesus Christ laid down His life for you, the door of grace is always open. You can go to your heavenly Father anytime and receive the gifts of forgiveness, reconciliation, and salvation.

BIBLE PROMISES FOR WHEN YOU'RE FEELING
Worthless

This world sometimes leaves us feeling kicked, empty, and wondering if it's all worth it—or if we are worth it. But God leaves no doubt of the tremendous value He places on every human life, including yours …

When You're Feeling Worthless

"So God created man in His own image;
in the image of God He created him;
male and female He created them."

~ Genesis 1:27 ~

*Your value begins with the fact
that you are made by the hand of
the Creator in His very image.*

"Can a woman forget her nursing
child, and not have compassion on
the son of her womb? Surely they may
forget, yet I will not forget you."

~ Isaiah 49:15 ~

*Even if you are forsaken by family
and friends, you are always
cherished in the heart of God.*

When You're Feeling Worthless

"For I know the thoughts that I think toward you, says the Lord, thoughts of peace and not of evil, to give you a future and a hope."

~ Jeremiah 29:11 ~

God's thoughts toward you are wonderful, and He has great plans for your life!

"Yes, I have loved you with an everlasting love; therefore with lovingkindness I have drawn you."

~ Jeremiah 31:3 ~

His love for you is relentless, immeasurable, and infinite.

WHEN YOU'RE FEELING WORTHLESS

"But God demonstrates His own love toward us, in that while we were still sinners, Christ died for us."

~ Romans 5:8 ~

Our Father in heaven loves you so intensely that He allowed His own Son to die in your place before you ever repented.

"Knowing that you were not redeemed with corruptible things, like silver or gold ... but with the precious blood of Christ."

~ 1 Peter 1:18, 19 ~

God was willing to pay the highest price in the universe to redeem you—the blood of His dear Son.

WHEN YOU'RE FEELING WORTHLESS

"Behold what manner of love the Father has bestowed on us, that we should be called children of God!"

~ 1 John 3:1 ~

God actually considers you His very own precious child.

"Now then, we are ambassadors for Christ, as though God were pleading through us"

~ 2 Corinthians 5:20 ~

God has given you a high calling as an ambassador to share His great love with others.

WHEN YOU'RE FEELING WORTHLESS

"But God, who is rich in mercy, because of His great love with which He loved us, even when we were dead in trespasses, made us alive together with Christ ... that in the ages to come He might show the exceeding riches of His grace in His kindness toward us in Christ Jesus."

~ Ephesians 2:5, 7 ~

Your heavenly Father has planned a magnificent, never-ending future for you.

When You're Feeling Worth...

"Therefore, if anyone is in Christ, he is a new creation; old things have passed away; behold, all things have become new."

~ 2 Corinthians 5:17 ~

If you belong to Jesus, you have a brand new, sparkling-clean life in Him.

. . . .

You belong to God, and as long as you cling to Him, no one can take that from you. His Word overwhelmingly confirms that you are His cherished treasure!

Bible Promises for When You Need Strength

This world generates endless challenges, some of which can sap our strength and leave us feeling drained and helpless. But you never need to feel powerless. Cherish these verses from God's Word...

When You Need Strength

"He gives power to the weak, and to those who have no might He increases strength. Even the youths shall faint and be weary, and the young men shall utterly fall, but those who wait on the Lord shall renew their strength."

~ Isaiah 40:29–31 ~

God will strengthen you if you simply lean on Him.

"The Lord is my strength and song, and He has become my salvation; He is my God, and I will praise Him."

~ Exodus 15:2 ~

You can always turn to the Source and find new strength in Him.

WHEN YOU NEED STRENGTH

"Be strong and of good courage, do not fear nor be afraid of them; for the L ORD your God, He is the One who goes with you. He will not leave you nor forsake you."

~ Deuteronomy 31:6 ~

With the Almighty God by your side, you are stronger than an army.

"I can do all things through Christ who strengthens me."

~ Philippians 4:13 ~

You can conquer any obstacle and overcome any problem as long as you cling to Jesus.

WHEN YOU NEED STRENGTH

"I will strengthen you, yes, I will help you, I will uphold you with My righteous right hand."

~ Isaiah 41:10 ~

The highest Power in the entire universe promises to continuously help and strengthen you!

"Be strong in the Lord and in the power of His might. Put on the whole armor of God, that you may be able to stand against the wiles of the devil."

~ Ephesians 6:10, 11 ~

The Lord wants to empower you today with His armor of truth, righteousness, the gospel of peace, faith, salvation, the Word of God, and prayer.

When You Need Strength

"Be of good courage, and He shall strengthen your heart, all you who hope in the Lord."

~ Psalm 31:24 ~

If you keep on trusting the Lord, drawing courage from Him and His Word, He will provide all the fortitude you need.

"And He said to me, 'My grace is sufficient for you, for My strength is made perfect in weakness.' Therefore most gladly I will rather boast in my infirmities, that the power of Christ may rest upon me. ... For when I am weak, then I am strong."

~ 2 Corinthians 12:9, 10 ~

When you recognize your own weakness, God can come in and fill you with His perfect strength.

WHEN YOU NEED STRENGTH

"The LORD is my rock and my fortress and my deliverer; my God, my strength, in whom I will trust; my shield and the horn of my salvation, my stronghold."

~ Psalm 18:2 ~

The Lord is your strength plus everything else that you need in every situation.

. . . .

Let the limitless power of God permeate your life today to encourage and strengthen you!

Bible Promises for When You Need Wisdom

Whether you're in the midst of a major decision or simply want to make the best day-to-day choices, wisdom is a necessity. According to Scripture, you can go to God at any time and receive the gift of wisdom from above. And, unlike the wisdom of this world, God's wisdom won't let you down! Consider His promises...

WHEN YOU NEED WISDOM

"The fear of the Lord is the beginning of wisdom; a good understanding have all those who do His commandments."

~ Psalm 111:10 ~

Wisdom starts with utmost respect for God and obedience to His uplifting commandments.

"If any of you lacks wisdom, let him ask of God, who gives to all liberally and without reproach, and it will be given to him."

~ James 1:5 ~

God has an unending supply of wisdom and is more than willing to give you all that you need today if you ask Him.

WHEN YOU NEED WISDOM

"Behold, You desire truth in the inward parts, and in the hidden part You will make me to know wisdom."

~ Psalm 51:6 ~

If you are honestly seeking God's will for your life, He will reveal His wisdom in your heart and mind.

"That the God of our Lord Jesus Christ, the Father of glory, may give to you the spirit of wisdom and revelation in the knowledge of Him."

~ Ephesians 1:17 ~

One of the most important applications of wisdom is to enhance your relationship with Jesus and your knowledge of Him.

When You Need Wisdom

"He stores up sound wisdom for the upright; He is a shield to those who walk uprightly."

~ Proverbs 2:7 ~

If you are living a life of righteousness in Christ, you can depend on God to provide an abundance of wisdom and keep you on the right track.

"But of Him you are in Christ Jesus, who became for us wisdom from God—and righteousness and sanctification and redemption."

~ 1 Corinthians 1:30 ~

Did you know Jesus became wisdom for you, and everything else that you need for salvation? What a wealth of wisdom is available through studying the life of Christ, who was filled with all wisdom!

When You Need Wisdom

"But it will turn out for you as an occasion for testimony. Therefore settle it in your hearts not to meditate beforehand on what you will answer; for I will give you a mouth and wisdom which all your adversaries will not be able to contradict or resist."

~ Luke 21:13–15 ~

If you rely on Him, God promises to give you such great wisdom when you witness for Him that those who oppose the truth will be silenced.

When You Need Wisdom

"The wisdom that is from above is first pure, then peaceable, gentle, willing to yield, full of mercy and good fruits, without partiality and without hypocrisy."

~ James 3:17 ~

The wisdom of this world is based in selfish desires and yields bitter fruit, but God's wisdom consists of the purest attributes and yields the happiest results.

. . . .

The God of all wisdom invites you to come to Him today and learn from Him. He is more than willing to guide every step you take and keep you on the path of salvation!

Bible Promises for When You're Feeling

Angry

It's one of the most common of human emotions, and sometimes there's good reason for it. Yet if uncontrolled, anger can be very damaging to your mental and spiritual well-being and even your physical health. Thankfully, God's Word gives great guidance regarding this powerful emotion, whether you are on the giving or receiving end…

WHEN YOU'RE FEELING ANGRY

"An angry man stirs up strife, and a furious man abounds in transgression."

~ Proverbs 29:22 ~

It's so easy to make a mistake when your heart is filled with rage, to do or say things you will later regret.

"'Be angry, and do not sin': do not let the sun go down on your wrath, nor give place to the devil."

~ Ephesians 4:26, 27 ~

Often, it takes time to cool down after your anger has peaked, but the Bible advises you to let go of your anger as soon as possible to keep from sinning.

WHEN YOU'RE FEELING ANGRY

"A fool vents all his feelings, but a wise man holds them back."

~ Proverbs 29:11 ~

Restraint will benefit you much more than unleashing your feelings of anger.

"A soft answer turns away wrath, but a harsh word stirs up anger."

~ Proverbs 15:1 ~

The next time someone comes at you with claws extended, try a gentle response.

When You're Feeling Angry

"He who is slow to anger is better than the mighty, and he who rules his spirit than he who takes a city."

~ Proverbs 16:32 ~

One of your most potent weapons against anger is the attribute of patience.

"The discretion of a man makes him slow to anger, and his glory is to overlook a transgression."

~ Proverbs 19:11 ~

It takes wisdom and strength from above to let the discourtesy and rudeness of others pass without retaliation.

When You're Feeling Angry

"A gift in secret pacifies anger, and a bribe behind the back, strong wrath."

~ Proverbs 21:14 ~

If someone with whom you were angry gave you a nice gift, might it soften your heart?

"Let every man be swift to hear, slow to speak, slow to wrath; for the wrath of man does not produce the righteousness of God."

~ James 1:19,20 ~

Here is the best reason for a follower of Christ to avoid anger.

WHEN YOU'RE FEELING ANGRY

"Rest in the L ORD, and wait patiently for Him; do not fret because of him who prospers in his way, because of the man who brings wicked schemes to pass. Cease from anger, and forsake wrath; do not fret—it only causes harm. For evildoers shall be cut off; but those who wait on the L ORD, they shall inherit the earth."

~ Psalm 37:7–9 ~

Even anger because of the temporary prosperity of the ungodly can have a negative effect on God's people and should be avoided.

When You're Feeling Angry

"But now you yourselves are to put off all these: anger, wrath, malice, blasphemy, filthy language out of your mouth."

~ Colossians 3:8 ~

Remember that every scriptural command is also a promise: God promises to give you the power to do what's right!

. . . .

God is ready and willing to help you conquer this potentially explosive emotion and defeat any unresolved anger in your life today!

Bible Promises for When You Are
Anxious

Worry and anxiety are all too common in our hurried, stressful, unpredictable lives. For some, anxiety is an infrequent occurrence; for others, it's a constant, distressing companion. Most of us fall somewhere in between. But God wants something better for us. You can claim these encouraging promises from your loving Father in heaven …

WHEN YOU ARE ANXIOUS

"Be anxious for nothing, but in everything by prayer and supplication, with thanksgiving, let your requests be made known to God; and the peace of God, which surpasses all understanding, will guard your hearts and minds through Christ Jesus."

~ Philippians 4:6, 7 ~

God invites you to come to Him with all your concerns and needs; He longs to help you find positive solutions to your problems.

When You Are Anxious

"Peace I leave with you, My peace I give to you; not as the world gives do I give to you. Let not your heart be troubled, neither let it be afraid."

~ John 14:27 ~

It's no ordinary peace Jesus offers you, but a powerful peace that works to eclipse your fear and anxiety.

"Trust in the Lord with all your heart, and lean not on your own understanding; in all your ways acknowledge Him, and He shall direct your paths."

~ Proverbs 3:5, 6 ~

If you're anxious over choices you must make, put your entire faith in the God of your life and He will steer you in the right direction.

When You Are Anxious

"Cast your burden on the LORD, and He shall sustain you; He shall never permit the righteous to be moved."

~ Psalm 55:22 ~

God wants you to lean on Him for support; He will carry all your burdens and keep you from slipping.

"And let the peace of God rule in your hearts, to which also you were called in one body; and be thankful."

~ Colossians 3:15 ~

God will drive out your anxious thoughts and fill your heart and mind with peace when you focus on Him.

WHEN YOU ARE ANXIOUS

"I will both lie down in peace,
and sleep; for You alone, O LORD,
make me dwell in safety."

~ Psalm 4:8 ~

A lack of proper rest only increases anxiety; trust your problems to the Lord and go to sleep knowing He is watching over you.

"Fear not, for I am with you; be
not dismayed, for I am your God.
I will strengthen you, yes, I will
help you, I will uphold you with
My righteous right hand."

~ Isaiah 41:10 ~

It's safe to release all your fears and worries into God's capable hands, knowing that He is right beside you, holding you up and providing the help and strength you need each day.

WHEN YOU ARE ANXIOUS

"And my God shall supply all
your need according to His riches
in glory by Christ Jesus."

~ Philippians 4:19 ~

*Worrying over material needs is a
waste of energy; our all-powerful God
owns the entire universe and will take
care of you—His precious child!*

. . . .

*Grasp the solid reassurance
in God's Word and know that
He will stay right with you
through any circumstances
life can throw your way!*

Bible Promises for When God Seems Distant

Probably all of us have had days when God seems especially far away. Even the psalmist David sometimes felt abandoned by God. Yet he wouldn't turn away from the Lord; instead, he would seek God more intensely. His faith paid off, and so will yours if you cling to God regardless of your feelings. Absorb these reassurances from His Word…

When God Seems Distant

"And those who know Your name will put their trust in You; for You, Lord, have not forsaken those who seek You."

~ Psalm 9:10 ~

If you are honestly seeking God, you can be sure He hasn't disowned you!

"Draw near to God and He will draw near to you."

~ James 4:8 ~

If you come to Him, the Lord is ready and willing to draw you into a closer relationship.

When God Seems Distant

"But from there you will seek the Lord your God, and you will find Him if you seek Him with all your heart and with all your soul."

~ Deuteronomy 4:29 ~

It takes willingness and effort on your part to seek God, but the Bible confirms that you will be greatly rewarded for that effort.

"For He Himself has said, 'I will never leave you nor forsake you.'"

~ Hebrews 13:5 ~

If you belong to Him, you will never be truly alone.

WHEN GOD SEEMS DISTANT

"The LORD of hosts is with us; the God of Jacob is our refuge."

~ Psalm 46:7 ~

The God of the entire universe stands with you and will help you!

"For the LORD will not cast off His people, nor will He forsake His inheritance."

~ Psalm 94:14 ~

It is God's desire and intention to save you; He's not in the business of throwing people away.

WHEN GOD SEEMS DISTANT

"The Lord is near to those who have a broken heart, and saves such as have a contrite spirit."

~ Psalm 34:18 ~

When you are at your weakest point, God is close by to help you.

"All that the Father gives Me will come to Me, and the one who comes to Me I will by no means cast out."

~ John 6:37 ~

If you have given your heart to Jesus, you can be sure He will never push you away.

When God Seems Distant

"Behold, I stand at the door and knock. If anyone hears My voice and opens the door, I will come in to him and dine with him, and he with Me."

~ Revelation 3:20 ~

Jesus knocks at your heart's door; have you invited Him in lately?

When God Seems Distant

"I am with you always, even to the end of the age."

~ Matthew 28:20 ~

If you are His follower, Christ's straightforward promise to you is that He will be with you and will see you through every aspect of your life until the very end of the world.

. . . .

Aren't you glad the Bible leaves no doubt on this subject? If you're seeking God, He is with you at all times, even when your emotional state makes it difficult to sense His presence. You are His beloved child!

Bible Promises for When You Are Scared

On this rapidly decaying planet where bad things happen 24/7, it's easy to get caught up in an unhealthy pattern of giving in to fearful thoughts. God doesn't want us to be controlled by fear. He desires that we conquer our fears by trusting in Him. Read His words …

WHEN YOU ARE SCARED

"I sought the Lord, and He heard me, and delivered me from all my fears."

~ Psalm 34:4 ~

If you seek His presence and His will, God will give you courage for whatever you face in life!

"But He said to them, 'Why are you fearful, O you of little faith?' Then He arose and rebuked the winds and the sea, and there was a great calm."

~ Matthew 8:26 ~

Jesus has the power to dispel your fears and bring a great calm to your life!

When You Are Scared

"Wait on the L<small>ORD</small>; be of good courage, and He shall strengthen your heart."

~ Psalm 27:14 ~

God is with you at all times and is a constant Source of strength!

"Do not be afraid of sudden terror, nor of trouble from the wicked when it comes; for the L<small>ORD</small> will be your confidence, and will keep your foot from being caught."

~ Proverbs 3:25,26 ~

Be assured that even in scary situations God is right beside you to help you.

When You Are Scared

"Peace I leave with you, My peace I give to you; not as the world gives do I give to you. Let not your heart be troubled, neither let it be afraid."

~ John 14:27 ~

If you let Him, Jesus will give you His peace that is more powerful than any fear.

"For God has not given us a spirit of fear, but of power and of love and of a sound mind."

~ 2 Timothy 1:7 ~

This is God's desire for all His children—hearts not controlled by fear but by His love and power, resulting in sensible, logical thoughts and cognitive clarity.

When You Are Scared

"God is our refuge and strength,
a very present help in trouble.
Therefore we will not fear, even
though the earth be removed."

~ Psalm 46:1, 2 ~

*Through tumultuous events, you can
put your faith in God; He will always be
with you and will be your security.*

"For you did not receive the spirit
of bondage again to fear, but you
received the Spirit of adoption by
whom we cry out, 'Abba, Father.'"

~ Romans 8:15 ~

*When you become a child of God,
He breaks those bonds of fear.*

WHEN YOU ARE SCARED

"There is no fear in love; but perfect love casts out fear."

~ 1 John 4:18 ~

Let God fill your heart with His love, keep focusing on Him, and your fears will fade away.

"The Lord is the strength of my life; of whom shall I be afraid?"

~ Psalm 27:1 ~

With the most powerful Being in the universe as your defender, you really have no one to fear.

. . . .

Why not bring your fears to God right now? His Word confirms that He longs to help you manage any fear in your life today!

Bible Promises for When You Are Worried About
the Future

Our largely unpredictable future and active imaginations often combine to cause us to fear what's ahead on the road of life. But your heavenly Father has the desire and power to chart a course for you that ultimately ends in joy. Read His promises …

When You Are Worried

"For I know the thoughts that I think toward you, says the Lord, thoughts of peace and not of evil, to give you a future and a hope."

~ Jeremiah 29:11 ~

There's no doubt that God has wonderful things in mind for your future!

"These things I have spoken to you, that in Me you may have peace. In the world you will have tribulation; but be of good cheer, I have overcome the world."

~ John 16:33 ~

Although this world is full of troubles, Jesus assures you He has conquered it all and will help you do the same.

WHEN YOU ARE WORRIED

"A man's heart plans his way, but the Lord directs his steps."

~ Proverbs 16:9 ~

You can be sure you're moving in the right direction only when you seek God's help.

"Teach me good judgment and knowledge, for I believe Your commandments."

~ Psalm 119:66 ~

God's Word and His commandments hold critical keys to making good decisions for your future.

WHEN YOU ARE WORRIED

"The LORD also will be a refuge for the oppressed, a refuge in times of trouble."

~ Psalm 9:9 ~

Whatever rough spots you encounter on your path, you can always hide yourself in Him.

"And in the days of these kings the God of heaven will set up a kingdom which shall never be destroyed … and it shall stand forever."

~ Daniel 2:44 ~

God's ultimate plan for your future is to save you in His eternal kingdom of love.

WHEN YOU ARE WORRIED

"For our citizenship is in heaven, from which we also eagerly wait for the Savior, the Lord Jesus Christ, who will transform our lowly body that it may be conformed to His glorious body."

~ Philippians 3:20, 21 ~

Jesus promises you a glorious future if you are faithful to Him.

WHEN YOU ARE WORRIED

"And God will wipe away every tear from their eyes; there shall be no more death, nor sorrow, nor crying. There shall be no more pain, for the former things have passed away."

~ Revelation 21:4 ~

God's deep desire is to give you a destiny overflowing with joy!

"You will guide me with Your counsel, and afterward receive me to glory."

~ Psalm 73:24 ~

God will show you the way, both in the present and into eternity, if you keep on trusting Him.

WHEN YOU ARE WORRIED

"I will instruct you and teach you in the way you should go; I will guide you with My eye."

~ Psalm 32:8 ~

God is the perfect GPS; if you depend on Him for guidance, you can't go wrong.

. . . .

God has promised to guide your steps and provide for your needs when you seek Him and His truth through His Word and trust in Him with all your heart. Will you choose to put Him first in your life today?

Bible Promises for When You Are *Grieving*

No one travels through life without, at some point, experiencing the loss of someone or something dear. The loss of a loved one through death is one of life's most intense challenges, and the pain can be overwhelming. But God doesn't leave you to suffer alone …

WHEN YOU ARE GRIEVING

"Surely He has borne our griefs and carried our sorrows; yet we esteemed Him stricken, smitten by God, and afflicted."

~ Isaiah 53:4 ~

Jesus, the greatest empathizer, understands what you are going through and will remain with you.

"Blessed are those who mourn, for they shall be comforted."

~ Matthew 5:4 ~

The Lord will wrap His arms of love and comfort around those who trust in Him.

When You Are Grieving

"He heals the brokenhearted
and binds up their wounds."

~ Psalm 147:3 ~

*Lean on God and allow Him to continue
the process of healing your broken heart.*

"Blessed be the God and Father of
our Lord Jesus Christ, the Father of
mercies and God of all comfort, who
comforts us in all our tribulation,
that we may be able to comfort
those who are in any trouble."

~ 2 Corinthians 1:3, 4 ~

Comforting you is God's specialty.

WHEN YOU ARE GRIEVING

❦

"Fear not, for I am with you; be not dismayed, for I am your God. I will strengthen you, yes, I will help you, I will uphold you with My righteous right hand."

~ Isaiah 41:10 ~

God promises to be with you and get you through this time of intense disappointment and loneliness.

"Yea, though I walk through the valley of the shadow of death, I will fear no evil; for You are with me; Your rod and Your staff, they comfort me."

~ Psalm 23:4 ~

Depend on His guidance to lead you out of that dark valley.

When You Are Grieving

"But I do not want you to be ignorant, brethren, concerning those who have fallen asleep, lest you sorrow as others who have no hope. For if we believe that Jesus died and rose again, even so God will bring with Him those who sleep in Jesus."

~ 1 Thessalonians 4:13, 14 ~

As believers, we have hope of the resurrection promised by God.

"And God will wipe away every tear from their eyes; there shall be no more death, nor sorrow, nor crying. There shall be no more pain, for the former things have passed away."

~ Revelation 21:4 ~

In the new earth that God has promised to create, He will dry your tears.

WHEN YOU ARE GRIEVING

"For the trumpet will sound, and the dead will be raised incorruptible, and we shall be changed. ... So when this corruptible has put on incorruption, and this mortal has put on immortality, then shall be brought to pass the saying that is written: 'Death is swallowed up in victory.'"

~ 1 Corinthians 15:52, 54 ~

At Christ's return, those who belong to Him will be raised and given life that will never end.

. . . .

Cling to the Lord and He will comfort you through the process of grieving and, in the future, will replace your sorrow with great, unending joy!

Bible Promises for When You Are Struggling
with Guilt

We all make mistakes, and God's Word says we all have sinned. No matter how you came to your situation or how long you've carried that distressing burden of guilt, God is ready with the solution. His arms are outstretched to you. Look at all He will do for you …

WHEN STRUGGLING WITH GUILT

"For God did not send His Son into the world to condemn the world, but that the world through Him might be saved."

~ John 3:17 ~

It's not God's purpose to condemn you; it's His desire to take away your sins and save you through Jesus Christ.

"For He made Him who knew no sin to be sin for us, that we might become the righteousness of God in Him."

~ 2 Corinthians 5:21 ~

Jesus not only died for your sins, He took your sins upon Himself so He could give you His righteousness— His right standing with God.

When Struggling with Guilt

"In Him we have redemption through His blood, the forgiveness of sins, according to the riches of His grace."

~ Ephesians 1:7 ~

Through the sacrificial death of Christ, you are given forgiveness and salvation as a free gift.

"'Come now, and let us reason together,' says the Lord, 'Though your sins are like scarlet, they shall be as white as snow; though they are red like crimson, they shall be as wool.'"

~ Isaiah 1:18 ~

God invites you to talk it over with Him, and He promises an outcome of great relief for you!

When Struggling with Guilt

"If we confess our sins, He is faithful and just to forgive us our sins and to cleanse us from all unrighteousness."

~ 1 John 1:9 ~

All you need to do is tell God where you went wrong, and He will take care of everything else and wash it all away.

"For I will be merciful to their unrighteousness, and their sins and their lawless deeds I will remember no more."

~ Hebrews 8:12 ~

In His great mercy, God erases your sin from His memory!

When Struggling with Guilt

"As far as the east is from the west, so far has He removed our transgressions from us."

~ Psalm 103:12 ~

It gives you a wonderful feeling of freedom to be separated from your sins.

"There is therefore now no condemnation to those who are in Christ Jesus, who do not walk according to the flesh, but according to the Spirit."

~ Romans 8:1 ~

If you follow Jesus and stay true to Him, you don't have to worry about the judgment; your guilt is a thing of the past.

WHEN STRUGGLING WITH GUILT

"Therefore, if anyone is in Christ, he is a new creation; old things have passed away; behold, all things have become new."

~ 2 Corinthians 5:17 ~

In addition to cleansing away all of your sins through the blood of the Lamb, God gives you a brand-new life!

. . . .

Why not go to God right now and accept His wonderful gift of forgiveness through Jesus Christ? You have nothing to lose and eternity to gain!

Bible Promises for When You're Feeling the Weight of the World on Your Shoulders

Life is tough, and the burdens it hands you can be so hard to bear. But you don't need to carry them alone...

For the Weight of the World

"Cast your burden on the Lord, and He shall sustain you; He shall never permit the righteous to be moved."

~ Psalm 55:22 ~

God is glad to carry your burdens and give you the daily strength you need.

"Is this not the fast that I have chosen: To loose the bonds of wickedness, to undo the heavy burdens, to let the oppressed go free, and that you break every yoke?"

~ Isaiah 58:6 ~

It's not God's will that you should be crushed down with excessive burdens; let Him free you today.

FOR THE WEIGHT OF THE WORLD

"Come to Me, all you who labor and are heavy laden, and I will give you rest. Take My yoke upon you and learn from Me, for I am gentle and lowly in heart, and you will find rest for your souls. For My yoke is easy and My burden is light."

~ Matthew 11:28–30 ~

Jesus will remove your heavy burden of guilt and hopelessness and give you true rest in Him.

For the Weight of the World

"For I, the Lord your God, will hold your right hand, saying to you, 'Fear not, I will help you.'"

~ Isaiah 41:13 ~

God promises to support and help you through every trial.

"Therefore humble yourselves under the mighty hand of God, that He may exalt you in due time, casting all your care upon Him, for He cares for you."

~ 1 Peter 5:6, 7 ~

Just knowing your heavenly Father cares about you personally can make any load seem lighter.

For the Weight of the World

"Even to your old age, I am He, and even to gray hairs I will carry you! I have made, and I will bear; even I will carry, and will deliver you."

~ Isaiah 46:4 ~

The Lord desires to constantly support you throughout your life, with the intention of saving you eternally.

"He will feed His flock like a shepherd; He will gather the lambs with His arm, and carry them in His bosom."

~ Isaiah 40:11 ~

The Good Shepherd will gladly bear you in His gentle arms right now.

FOR THE WEIGHT OF THE WORLD

"The righteous cry out, and the LORD hears, and delivers them out of all their troubles."

~ Psalm 34:17 ~

If you belong to Him, God will always listen when you call to Him for help.

"Bear one another's burdens, and so fulfill the law of Christ."

~ Galatians 6:2 ~

When God has lightened your burdens, He asks you to do the same for others.

For the Weight of the World

"When you pass through the waters, I will be with you; and through the rivers, they shall not overflow you. ... Fear not, for I am with you"

~ Isaiah 43:2, 5 ~

Through faith His strength becomes yours, and He reaches out to keep you from falling.

. . . .

Why not come to Jesus today and allow Him to relieve you of your heavy load?

Bible Promises for When You Are
Feeling Lonely

Are you feeling lonely? It's strange that, at times, one can be surrounded by people and still feel very alone. You can feel lonely even among people who love you; they may not understand what you're going through, at least not fully. But there is Someone who understands your heart completely. He knows your thoughts, feels your every emotion, and longs for you to know He's with you and for you. Take comfort in His promises …

When You Are Feeling Lonely

"And I will pray the Father, and He will give you another Helper, that He may abide with you forever—the Spirit of truth.... I will not leave you orphans; I will come to you."

~ John 14:16–18 ~

You never need to feel abandoned because Jesus promised to be right there with you; He will even be, through His Holy Spirit, in you.

"God is our refuge and strength, a very present help in trouble."

~ Psalm 46:1 ~

So many troubling situations in life can leave you feeling alone and insecure, but God is a "very present help" at all times.

WHEN YOU ARE FEELING LONELY

"When my father and my mother forsake me, then the Lord will take care of me."

~ Psalm 27:10 ~

Even when those closest to your heart turn away, the God of love will remain with you, safeguard you, and tenderly look after your needs.

"I am with you always, even to the end of the age."

~ Matthew 28:20 ~

As long as you desire His presence, there will never come a time when God will leave you to fend for yourself.

When You Are Feeling Lonely

"He heals the brokenhearted
and binds up their wounds."

~ Psalm 147:3 ~

Sometimes it's a broken heart that leaves you feeling lonely, but the Lord promises to heal the wounds and hold you close to Him.

"'For the mountains shall depart
and the hills be removed, but My
kindness shall not depart from you,
nor shall My covenant of peace
be removed,' says the Lord."

~ Isaiah 54:10 ~

God is so faithful that you can depend on His care and attention even if the mountains crumble around you!

WHEN YOU ARE FEELING LONELY

"In my distress I called upon the Lord, and cried out to my God; He heard my voice from His temple, and my cry came before Him, even to His ears."

~ Psalm 18:6 ~

You never have to feel that no one hears you, because your heavenly Father always hears and understands.

"For I, the Lord your God, will hold your right hand, saying to you, 'Fear not, I will help you.'"

~ Isaiah 41:13 ~

Loneliness will vanish when you realize the Almighty God is holding your hand!

When You Are Feeling Lonely

"Be strong and of good courage ... for the LORD your God, He is the One who goes with you. He will not leave you nor forsake you."

~ Deuteronomy 31:6 ~

The Creator of the universe is on your team, and He will never leave you!

. . . .

Be encouraged in the loving presence of your Savior, knowing He will always stand beside you. And why not share these verses with someone you love?

Bible Promises for When You've Hit Rock Bottom

So many circumstances in life can leave us feeling discouraged and helpless. But there's good reason to be optimistic; there's One who cares deeply about you. Read His promises …

When You've Hit Rock Bottom

"Call upon Me in the day of trouble; I will deliver you, and you shall glorify Me."

~ Psalm 50:15 ~

The Lord is unlimited in His ability to rescue you from any problem.

"Why are you cast down, O my soul? And why are you disquieted within me? Hope in God, for I shall yet praise Him for the help of His countenance."

~ Psalm 42:5 ~

Your heavenly Father is the source of all hope and is eager to help you.

WHEN YOU'VE HIT ROCK BOTTOM

"He shall cover you with His feathers, and under His wings you shall take refuge; His truth shall be your shield and buckler."

~ Psalm 91:4 ~

In drawing close to God and seeking truth from His Word, you will find comfort and protection.

"You are my strong refuge."

~ Psalm 71:7 ~

You never need to feel alone with the all-powerful God of the universe by your side.

WHEN YOU'VE HIT ROCK BOTTOM

"For He will deliver the needy when he cries, the poor also, and him who has no helper."

~ Psalm 72:12 ~

God is the Helper of the helpless and loves to rescue those who call on Him.

"From the end of the earth I will cry to You, when my heart is overwhelmed; lead me to the rock that is higher than I."

~ Psalm 61:2 ~

Ask God for help, and He will guide you to an immovable foundation.

When You've Hit Rock Bottom

"Trust in the LORD with all your heart, and lean not on your own understanding; in all your ways acknowledge Him, and He shall direct your paths."

~ Proverbs 3:5, 6 ~

Lean totally on Him, look to Him for guidance, and He will show you what you need to do next.

"For consider Him who endured such hostility from sinners against Himself, lest you become weary and discouraged in your souls. You have not yet resisted to bloodshed, striving against sin."

~ Hebrews 12:3, 4 ~

The One who purposefully shed His blood for you understands what you are going through.

When You've Hit Rock Bottom

"He also brought me up out of a horrible pit, out of the miry clay, and set my feet upon a rock, and established my steps."

~ Psalm 40:2 ~

As dreadful as your circumstances may appear, God has a perfect plan to get you back on solid ground.

"I am with you always, even to the end of the age."

~ Matthew 28:20 ~

Jesus promises to accompany you through every circumstance of life.

When You've Hit Rock Bottom

**"He who has begun a good work
in you will complete it until
the day of Jesus Christ."**

~ Philippians 1:6 ~

*God fully intends to save you in His kingdom
of love; He isn't going to give up on you!*

. . . .

*Cry out to the Lord, trust in Him, lean
on Him, seek Him with all your being,
wait patiently on Him, and He will help
you conquer every difficulty you face!*

Bible Promises for When You Are Feeling
Stressed

Nearly everyone experiences some level of stress on a daily basis, and sometimes it can get out of hand. Thankfully, God's Word gives helpful direction on how to find relief for whatever is pressuring you ...

When You Are Feeling Stressed

> "I have set the LORD always before me; because He is at my right hand I shall not be moved."

~ Psalm 16:8 ~

Know first that God is with you at all times and is watching over you.

> "Be still, and know that I am God."

~ Psalm 46:10 ~

Do you ever find the frantic rush of life eclipsing your focus on God and His Word? It's critical to take time for quietness with Him.

When You Are Feeling Stressed

"Be anxious for nothing, but in everything by prayer and supplication, with thanksgiving, let your requests be made known to God; and the peace of God, which surpasses all understanding, will guard your hearts and minds through Christ Jesus."

~ Philippians 4:6, 7 ~

After you've listened for His still small voice, tell your heavenly Father exactly what you need, and receive His immeasurable peace.

WHEN YOU ARE FEELING STRESSED

"Take My yoke upon you and learn from Me, for I am gentle and lowly in heart, and you will find rest for your souls."

~ Matthew 11:29 ~

If you seek Christ and live in obedience to Him, He will give you calming rest.

"You will keep him in perfect peace, whose mind is stayed on You, because he trusts in You."

~ Isaiah 26:3 ~

Focusing on God and trusting in Him results in His perfect peace expanding in your heart.

WHEN YOU ARE FEELING STRESSED

"Better a handful with quietness than both hands full, together with toil and grasping for the wind."

~ Ecclesiastes 4:6 ~

Being thankful and content with what you have is another key to beating stress.

"Remember the Sabbath day, to keep it holy."

~ Exodus 20:8 ~

Observing the weekly seventh-day Sabbath and keeping it holy is one of the greatest blessings and de-stressors God has given to mankind!

When You Are Feeling Stressed

"My brethren, count it all joy when you fall into various trials, knowing that the testing of your faith produces patience. But let patience have its perfect work, that you may be perfect and complete, lacking nothing."

~ James 1:2–4 ~

If you find yourself in the midst of trouble, be patient and remember that God has the power to bring good things even from your trials.

"Then He arose and rebuked the wind, and said to the sea, 'Peace, be still!' And the wind ceased and there was a great calm."

~ Mark 4:39 ~

Just as Jesus quieted the storm at sea, He will gladly quiet your anxious thoughts and soothe your troubled mind!

WHEN YOU ARE FEELING STRESSED

"And He said to them, 'Come aside by yourselves to a deserted place and rest a while.' For there were many coming and going, and they did not even have time to eat."

~ Mark 6:31 ~

As Jesus' disciple, you need regular times of re-creation and rest to maintain good physical and emotional health.

. . . .

Why not ask your loving Savior right now to carry your burdens and quiet you with His infinite love?

Bible Promises for When You Feel Tempted

Temptation happens regularly to all of us. Remember, there's nothing wrong in being tempted. After all, even Jesus was tempted, but of course He overcame each temptation. It's only when we give in to the temptation that we fail, but that never needs to happen. Read on and hold tight to His promises …

WHEN YOU FEEL TEMPTED

"For in that He Himself has suffered, being tempted, He is able to aid those who are tempted."

~ Hebrews 2:18 ~

Jesus understands from experience what you are facing and will help you get through it victoriously if you trust in Him.

"You are of God, little children, and have overcome them, because He who is in you is greater than he who is in the world."

~ 1 John 4:4 ~

It's not your strength that matters, but the strength of Christ in you!

When You Feel Tempted

"No temptation has overtaken you except such as is common to man; but God is faithful, who will not allow you to be tempted beyond what you are able, but with the temptation will also make the way of escape."

~ 1 Corinthians 10:13 ~

You may think you suffer alone in a particular temptation, but you can be sure others have been there; with God's help you'll find a way out!

"Therefore let him who thinks he stands take heed lest he fall."

~ 1 Corinthians 10:12 ~

When things are going smoothly, it's easy to fall into a pattern of putting trust in yourself; that's when you're most vulnerable to temptation.

WHEN YOU FEEL TEMPTED

"Therefore submit to God. Resist the devil and he will flee from you. Draw near to God and He will draw near to you."

~ James 4:7, 8 ~

Your part in overcoming temptation is to resist it and to seek God with all your heart!

"Your word I have hidden in my heart, that I might not sin against You."

~ Psalm 119:11 ~

Fill your mind with Scripture and those verses will return to support you just when you need them most; this is how Jesus defeated temptation!

When You Feel Tempted

"Be strong in the Lord and in the power of His might. Put on the whole armor of God, that you may be able to stand against the wiles of the devil."

~ Ephesians 6:10, 11 ~

You can never stand against the enemy in your own strength, but Jesus offers you His strength to resist temptation.

"Now to Him who is able to keep you from stumbling, and to present you faultless before the presence of His glory with exceeding joy."

~ Jude 1:24 ~

God won't give up on you; He wants you with Him forever!

When You Feel Tempted

———— ✦ ————

"These things I write to you, so that you may not sin. And if anyone sins, we have an Advocate with the Father, Jesus Christ the righteous."

~ 1 John 2:1 ~

If you fall, don't be discouraged; God promises you forgiveness and a fresh start through Jesus Christ!

. . . .

The One who overcame all temptation to win eternal life for you, also promises He will be with you each day and give you the strength to win every battle!

Bible Promises for When You Feel That No One Cares

The world can be such an uncaring place, and circumstances can leave you feeling cold, empty, and alone. Sometimes it's easy to forget that God loves you personally and deeply and cares very much about your welfare. Look at His uplifting words for you …

When You Feel That No One Cares

"For I know the thoughts that I think toward you, says the Lord, thoughts of peace and not of evil, to give you a future and a hope."

~ Jeremiah 29:11 ~

Whatever your situation right now, God is for you and has wonderful plans for your life.

"The one who comes to Me I will by no means cast out."

~ John 6:37 ~

Regardless of your past, the arms of the Savior are outstretched to you in welcome.

When You Feel That No One Cares

> "The eternal God is your refuge, and underneath are the everlasting arms."

~ Deuteronomy 33:27 ~

The Lord will shelter you from the harshness of this world, supporting you with His arms of love.

> "The LORD is near to those who have a broken heart, and saves such as have a contrite spirit."

~ Psalm 34:18 ~

If your heart is broken today, be assured that God understands and is right there with you, desiring to heal your wounded spirit.

When You Feel That No One Cares

"Blessed be the God and Father of our Lord Jesus Christ, the Father of mercies and God of all comfort, who comforts us in all our tribulation."

~ 2 Corinthians 1:3,4 ~

His mercy toward you is unfathomable, and He is always ready to comfort you in whatever you are experiencing.

# When You Feel That No One Cares

> "Casting all your care upon
> Him, for He cares for you."

~ 1 Peter 5:7 ~

*God doesn't turn away when you unload
your burdens on Him; even if all your
friends and family were to abandon
you, God would still care for you.*

> "I have loved you with an
> everlasting love; therefore with
> lovingkindness I have drawn you."

~ Jeremiah 31:3 ~

*God's love for you is limitless;
He loves you forever!*

When You Feel That No One Cares

"For He Himself has said, 'I will never leave you nor forsake you.'"

~ Hebrews 13:5 ~

Jesus, who died to save you, is more faithful than any earthly friend, and He promised to stay beside you always.

"Behold what manner of love the Father has bestowed on us, that we should be called children of God!"

~ 1 John 3:1 ~

When you come to God, you become part of His family of love and God accepts you as His own child!

When You Feel That No One Cares

> "He shall cover you with His feathers, and under His wings you shall take refuge; His truth shall be your shield and buckler."

~ Psalm 91:4 ~

If you seek God and trust in Him, He will defend you just as a protective eagle parent that spreads its wings over its chicks.

. . . .

Whatever you are facing today, know that God's heart overflows with love and concern for you and that He will stay with you and help you through any difficulty.

When You Need
BIBLE TRUTH

Bible knowledge brings peace, hope, and happiness. That's why we invite you to explore these incredible websites full of trustworthy information about the Bible—you will be wowed and blessed with every click!

....

TruthAboutDeath.com
What really happens when we die? Explore what the Bible really has to say—you'll be amazed and blessed and encouraged with the truth!

SabbathTruth.com
God has designed a special day for all mankind. What happened to that day? How can you receive the promises of it today? The truth is just around the corner!

HellTruth.com
What the Bible really says about hellfire will amaze you and bring you peace and comfort. A true understanding about hell will transform your understanding of God.

GhostTruth.com
What does the Bible say about ghosts? The Bible truth is so important that you simply don't want to miss visiting this website!

666Truth.com
A lot of misinformation about the mark of the beast is circulating through the Christian church! Get a Bible-based perspective that actually makes sense!

BibleProphecyTruth.com
Do you want to better understand Bible prophecy and how it affects you? Then don't wait to visit this vast website full of prophecy information you can trust!

Explore the Bible in-depth at these sites ...

AmazingFacts.org
BibleHistory.com
BibleUniverse.com
ProphecySeminars.com

Follow us on Facebook, Twitter, and YouTube!

Promises for
Your Future

Discover incredible truth about God's Word and the last days of earth's history with Amazing Facts' Bible Study Guide series. Increase your Bible knowledge exponentially—and be inspired by God's great love through these 27 in-depth, exciting lessons.

Visit online at
www.amazingfacts.org
today and discover:

- What happens after death
- The way to better health
- How to save your marriage
- The truth about hell fire
and many other amazing facts!

Or send for the printed guides absolutely **FREE!** Send your name and mailing address to the address below, and indicate that you would like to begin the Bible Study course.

Amazing Facts • P.O. Box 909 • Roseville, CA 95678

Free offer available in North America and U.S. territories only.

Do you want promises for BETTER HEALTH?

Amazing Health Facts Magazine

This attractive, affordable, full-color magazine presents eight powerful biblical health lessons in a direct and captivating way — including the benefits of a good diet, exercise, rest and the Sabbath, sunlight, water, and more.

- Over 50 pages of health information developed by medical professionals
- Features hundreds of eye-catching graphics and amazing health facts
- Is perfect for evangelism and priced for mass sharing

Use code BK-AHF
Bulk Pricing Available!

Only $2.50

To order call **800-538-7275** or visit **www.afbookstore.com**

MORE GREAT RESOURCES FROM AMAZING FACTS

365 Amazing Answers to Big Bible Questions
A Daily Devotional

This daily devotional covers the most frequently asked Bible questions from Pastor Doug's *Bible Answers Live* program. The direct, concise answers cover topics on lifestyle, doctrine, history, prophecy, and specific passages of Scripture. QR codes are included to link you to related content on one of our many Amazing Facts websites! Enhance your devotional time and find big answers to questions in your life. A valuable addition to your study library for years to come!
BK-AADD ... $19.95

The Book of Amazing Facts, Volumes 1 & 2

Doug Batchelor. Enjoy Pastor Doug's popular amazing facts now collected into these two incredible volumes! Whether you're preparing a sermon, need an attention grabber for a children's story, or just enjoy fascinating trivia, these books are a wonderful resource!
AF-BOAF ... $12.95
AF-BOAF2 ... $12.95

Order today at AFBOOKSTORE.COM

A World of Wonders
A Daily Devotional
Enjoy Pastor Doug's first-ever daily devotional! Drawing from history, nature, science, and technology, these 366 devotionals provide fascinating facts and powerful spiritual messages. Teens and kids will love the concise and interesting entries!
AF-WGDD ... $19.95

NKJV Prophecy Study Bibles
These brilliant study Bibles from Amazing Facts combine the easy-to-understand language and accuracy of the New King James Version with a special emphasis on prophecy to supercharge your spiritual life! Loaded with helpful features: all 27 Amazing Facts Study Guides, The Biblical Cyclopedic Index, 64-page Concordance, Words of Christ in Red, Doug Batchelor's "Studying the Bible," and much more!

<u>Giant Print Premium Leather</u>
BK-PSBGPL ... $99.95

<u>Navy Blue Leathersoft</u> (Sword)
BK-PSBNL ... $76.95

<u>Teal Leathersoft</u> (Floral Pattern)
BK-PSBTL ... $76.95

Prices subject to change.

or call **800-538-7275**